N O T A M O M E N T T O O S O O N

Frank Kuppner was born in Glasgow in 1951. He has written eleven Carcanet collections. The first, *A Bad Day for the Sung Dynasty*, was awarded a Scottish Arts Council Book award in 1984. *Second Best Moments in Chinese History* received the same award in 1997. A novelist as well as a poet, he received the McVitie's Prize for his fiction in 1995. He has been Writer in Residence at the universities of Edinburgh, Strathclyde and Glasgow.

NOT

frAnk kuppner

CARCANET POETRY

A MOMENT TOO SOON

First published in Great Britain in 2024 by
Carcanet
Alliance House, 30 Cross Street
Manchester, M2 7AQ
www.carcanet.co.uk

A CIP catalogue record for this book is
available from the British Library.

ISBN 978 1 80017 398 9

Book design by Andrew Latimer, Carcanet
Typesetting by LiteBook Prepress Services
Printed in Great Britain by SRP Ltd, Exeter, Devon

The publisher acknowledges financial
assistance from Arts Council England.

CONTENTS

TAWA
"Can we be led life
enhancingly towards the
Unbearable Truth?"

[Well, actually, I meant "TAWH" – but "TAWA"
would no doubt do perfectly well instead]

NOT A MOMENT TOO SOON

THE LIBERATING VERTIGO OF A FINAL PASSAGE OF MEANING

ONE

1.
Of course there is no
correct final order for
the World to assume.

2.
Points weaved together
to make myself – (hello?) – then
on to other things…

3.
Sometimes I watch my
hand writing – but I'm still not
entirely convinced.

4.
No. I too can't quite
grasp the sense of a self   which
has emerged like this.

5.
Perhaps the whole world
is not *really* like what it
so clearly *is* like?

6.
"Life is rarely quite
what one expects – even if
one knows what's coming."

7.
Non-existence seems
to have badly lost control
of the whole business.

8.
This fitful fever –
with the odd request for a
birth certificate.

9.
Through the Dantean
dark woods blow pages torn from
fashion magazines!

10.
It flared for a brief
shining moment in the sky,
whatever it was.

11.
How can it make me
so happy to reach these dull
ordinary sta[i]rs?

12.
I'm guessing. It may
be that star there. Or, perhaps,
the one next to it.

13.
A muted quarrel
comes up the stairway, pauses –
then goes in next door.

14.

I'm here now – but that
would simply not be the case
if I were elsewhere.

15.

(Having reached the peak,
we nonetheless decided
to keep on climbing.)

16.

The absurd striving
for something else beyond the
limitlessly real.

17.

As if all were on
a boundless surface, but the
surface is too deep.

18.

And, all the time, this
relentless, mindless churning
far below our feet…

19.

I don't know. All these
stars, planets, and so forth, just
don't feel *safe* somehow.

20.

If the Sun were to
explode – (but, no… it's doing
just that already.)

21.

(These restless seconds –
all of them sure to vanish
eventually…)

22.

I'm told there was a
once-in-a-lifetime eclipse
a few days ago?

23.

How unlike a crab
it scuttles across the sky
waving its bright claw!

24.

Through a skylight which
he hadn't noticed before
there came no moonlight.

25.

Perhaps it's the sweep
of the light from this cheap lamp
that does most of it?

26.

The church-spire's shadow
now blocks out half the room.
⠀⠀⠀⠀⠀I'll
need to move my chair.

27.

The light effect banged
off various walls, before
noticing the door.

28.

For a moment, I
couldn't tell whether it was
sunlight or gold paint.

29.

A rat carefully
crossing the superb floor of
a darkened temple...

30.

Whatever it is,
it's been spreading over the
lawn for a while now.

31.

In glorious bloom
over millions of years – yet
never once admired!

32.

One of the deckchairs
sank to earth shortly after
both the guests had left.

33.

A bird lands, looks round,
then flies off – since all we are
is two more details.

34.

A leaf flew in through
the window... and landed on
whatever was there.

35.
Still... fairly soon, it
got back onto its feet, looked
round, then hurried off.

36.
So many aspects
of this room must once have been
widely spaced-out trees.

37.
A vast squall of leaves
blowing over the slope, more
or less forever.

38.
Leaves whirling about
in the grounds of the vanished
Children's Hospital.

39.
So many children
we never had, darling – if
I may call you that.

40.
Or one of my own
parents might have passed *you* in
the street, unnoticed.

41.
Doing all we can
to sound like proper adults
to the very end!

42.
A simple request
reached across the centuries
and opened this door.

43.
These eerie feelings –
whatever they mean – go back
for millions of years.

44.
I switched on the lamp
and said a few words which I
felt *had* to be said.

45.
There's that light again,
far off high among the trees
of the park at dusk!

46.
One by one, the lights
go out, and the more
       intense
conversations start.

47.
Night. A brief light shines
in the building we had thought
long since derelict.

48.
The last light ebbs, and
a few million sighs weigh
        down
the fading grey clouds.

49.
The lights go out, and
countless universes are
gently laid aside.

50.
Off they go, branching
back, often intermingling
with their own dead weeds.

51.
Such a dangerous
world! – and with so much *sleeping*
going on in it –

52.
Hmm. That's a highly
unusual position
to fall asleep in.

53.
They look to me like
failed women. *Narrowly* failed,
perhaps. But, still… *failed.*

54.
For half an hour, I've
just been sitting here thinking
about Piltdown Man.

55.
In my dreams, I talk
to people who (perhaps) I
should talk to much more.

TWO

1.
An old friend, long dead,
making some fresh, new, witty
remarks in a dream.

2.
"I've often thought I
would rather like to be one
of these wayside shrines."

3.
There used to be a
small statue near that garage.
Yes. Venus, I think.

4.
Then a large statue
of a god's mother farted
and fell to pieces.

5.
Surely there can be
nothing *ultimate* about
anthropomorphism?

6.
No. Even one arm
reaching out of the sky would
be one too many.

7.
"This is not something
which I had quite expected
to not happen twice."

8.
Is that the same cat
that was here last night? It looks
a good bit *bigger*.

9.
Put that one there and
that one back there. Right. Good. What
do you think of that?

10.
Though the god had died
his penis kept lengthening
for the next few days.

11.
Good Heavens! It turns
out that Almighty God was
quite right after all!

12.
Glory be to that
for so many cries of pain
which help fill our lives.

13.

Such hordes of microbes
working away at their tasks
during Christ's lifetime!

14.

I nearly had this
same operation over
fifty years ago.

15.

Efflorescences
of microbial life take
in our history.

16.

It was the last thing
I expected to see from
a hospital bed.

17.

"I would prefer all
this to have happened without
grief, loss and so forth."

18.

Complex atomic
structures, caught up in such vast
local confusions!

19.

Does existential
superfluousness turn out
something lovable?

20.

How one still awaits
one's apology from the
Universe as such...

21.

Whatever this is –
how can it possibly have
happened to me too?

22.

Non-existence seems
to be an even weaker
cage than existence.

23.

Yes. Non-existence
too evidently ended,
darling, in failure.

24.

How like the *All*, Sir,
your work is! (In no sense a
product of genius.)

25.

But who has yet said
a truly revealing word
about Nothingness?

26.

Drifting through all these
particles as if we had
nothing in common!

27.

All that real love – and
off it drifts into the stars.
Heat. Starlight. Gases.

28.

All that space for the
Earth to move through? Perhaps a
little excessive?

29.

If that swarm of stars
were nearer – would we not (here
too) be used to them?

30.

I dare say we could
have looked at those dots for a
bit longer last night.

31.

Some things in my eyes
are dried blood – while others are
a world beyond them.

32.

Two days after I'd
read some Kafka parables,
my eye[s] haemorrhaged.

33.

I lost a *huge* map
of some city or other
in my dreams last night.

34.
"This street used to be
wildly busy – when it was
a *real* street, of course."

35.
A f[r]og slipped out and
paused at the kerb, shouting "Which
way to the Castle?"

36.
Being a tree would
perhaps be all right if one
could still walk about…

37.
How can such clearly
absurd forms of life fit in
so seamlessly here?

38.
Flying about all
over the place – frequently
landing on rooftops…

39.
What? Only one of
all the world's arms is easing
this throbbing shoulder?

40.
"Oh, I know I'd *hate*
to spend my life in a cave,
hanging upside-down!"

41
Are those the remnants
of a living thing up there
among the cobwebs?

42.
So much loose liquid
falling from the skies, as if
that was simply that…

43.
Those small black marks on
our kitchen wall… surely they're
not also alive?

44.
I had such high hopes
for that cushion with the print
of Loch Ness on it.

45.
Remind me again:
What is Saint Arsenius
the Patron Saint *of?*

46.
Avoiding a world
which was only just reached in
an endless crisis…

47.
A large bright feather
has somehow arrived at our
front door overnight!

48.
Somebody's lipstick
lying beneath a small bench
in the bus station.

49.
Bliss on a path which
I took simply to avoid
some churned ruts of mud.

50.
Those charmed creatures which
always elude capture are
now back in this room!

51.
Good Heavens! Has there
always been this small bright *glade*
halfway down our lane?

52.
That's the house where I'd
like to die – if I could just
get in there somehow…

53.
As the bus pulls out
we glimpse our own
             windows down
one of the side-streets.

54.
Was that white flash back
there – a house? Yes? Maybe with
someone *real* inside?

55.
As the years passed, I
grew more like my real self – to
some extent at least.

56.
The endless world at
present contains this date – (which
I shall now devour)

57.
It rolled out of the
school and went some way down the
fairly level street.

58.
Those coins we left on
a park bench are no doubt still
in circulation.

59.
When I went back out
to bring in the last chair – it
had already gone!

60.
"I've only once had
to slip an oil-painting out
through a back-window."

61.

The oceans must be
pretty full of musical
instruments by now?

62.

"My God! What an arse!"
I thought as I speechlessly
left the Concert Hall.

63.

Another huge crowd
disperses. (Next week's huge crowd
should be here next week.)

64.

Two strange light scrape-marks
have somehow appeared at our
front door overnight.

65.

Detached from a world
which we reached only with such
vast difficulty!

66.

A hat careering
across the flustered street with
no-one chasing it.

67.

Hailstones! What more proof
do we need, that the whole thing
is not about us?

68.

What indifference
the sea would be showing us
if it had feelings.

69.

Mere passions that don't
last? Well – how did most of us
get here anyway?

70.

"Save yourselves!" screams the
Universe as such (though it's
not quite clear to whom.)

71.

"It's going to be
all right in the end," lied a
weak voice in the dust.

72.

"Yes," said God. "And that
surely gives us a really
nice note to end on."

73.

Right. Fine. That is that.
Nothing is ever going
to happen again.

74.

"What's the point of it?"
thought God to himself. "What CAN
the point of it be?"

75.

Millions of years pass –
before the fatal mountain
is declared sacred.

76.

The ancient temple
is encrusted with shit – (no
doubt, mainly from birds.)

77.

Dawn. And I must now
proceed on its way to the
dream-filled abattoir.

78.

Are we still alive?
My God – what a collusion!
(If that's quite the word?)

79.

What a life I've had!
(Yes. Whether me – or someone
absurdly *like* me.)

80.

If I were someone
else… [Well… what would this person
prefer to add here?]

81.

What? I've just thought of
a brief phrase which describes *the
whole thing* perfectly!

82.

Morning. More shadows
creep out into pathways of
unknowable lives.

83.

So like Everything –
drifting about as if it
had no past at all.

NOT QUITE THE GREATEST STORY NEVER TOLD

1.
Compared to what is
the universe important –
or [indeed] unimportant?

2.
"Right! Time to whip out
this tool and set to work. There!
Now I've begun it."

[The obvious place to start.

(For a moment I actually thought of calling it 'The Creator *Lied!*')

(Obviously inadequate.)]

3.
I was going to
do something just then – but what
was it? What was it?

[Replace the final phrases with
both *What is it?* and *What wasn't?*]

4.
And thus I woke up
into another morning
of divine failure.

5.

It's not really a
convincing alternative
to non-existence. [Is it?]

6.

("There's something a touch
unnatural, Eve, about
existence as such.")

['Perhaps non-existence is the only
sure way of not being annihilated.'
(*Cant*)]
[Unless it was someone else!]
[But is it a price worth paying my
angel –

7.

A joke taken too
seriously? A clear point
marvellously missed?

8.

"Oh, it's quite simple.
The universe as such is
not under control."

9.

Suddenly the plan[e]t
burst into flames – shaking no
vacant onlookers.

10.

"But then – so much is
almost inevitable –
isn't it, Sy[la]bil?"

11.

("It's no good. We can't
keep our hands off each other,"
laughed the Almighty.)

12.

Next day, the whole thing
caught fire – which came as rather
a shock to us all.

['to *them* all', surely?]

13.

Flukes out of flukes, in
all directions – multiply –
good and bad alike!

14.

(How did it begin?
I'm not quite sure. In fact – did
it begin at all?)

15.

"Good day! Yes. I'm as
real as you are. Do you have
a problem with that?"

[("Because, for much of the time, I myself certainly do!")

Notgod speaking?]

16.

Far too much nonsense
falls from the sky! (Why can't it
just stay where it is?)

17.

No. Not much more than
a few shameful hairs drifting
along through the stars…

18.

Our most sacred noise
is one more guise that gases
briefly change[d] into.

19.

What can these clouds do?
Well – what did the last crowd do?
Do we have to watch?

20.

Oh, for God's sake! Is
that *another* one on this
quiet forest path?

21.

In unseen drawers,
so many collections of
similar treasures…

[Or *heads*.]

22.

Don't they all grow tired
of not looking for something
which is not quite here?

[An earlier version?]

23.

It's a great name for
a tiny mark on the hide
of the universe!

24.

Weeds keep cropping up
here and there. As, indeed, do
so many [other] life-forms.

25.

Something uncanny
is clearly just about to
happen in this space.

26.

What plank is that which
keeps trying to climb in through
the kitchen window?

[An obvious mispring.

Presumably 'plant' was intended – rather than, say, 'plane'.
   (Though, for that matter, the simple 'plan' is also extremely
   tempting – O my [broadly speaking, to some extent at least]
   more or less incomparable double and life-companion!)]

27.
I recognise this,
I thought – quite mistakenly,
as it now turns out...

28.
"The crowning glory
of lizards surely is that
they are not insects?"

[Or flowers, of course.]

29.
What rare promise seems
not quite able to break in
through this bright window!

30.
Light pulses forward
somewhere in a callous heart
from another world.

[Careless?]

31.
[*That's never going*
(I suddenly realised)
to happen, is it?]

32.
"Somehow it appears
I have quietly drifted
apart from myself."

[(God?) But, very likely we are
all somehow partly impersonating
ourselves – rarely, at a guess,
too well or convincingly.]

33.
"We're nearly too old
for this sort of thing," I said.
And both of us smiled.

34.
"Well – yes. More or less
everything has to be
the end of something."

[An unforgettable voice.]

35.
A sigh as I reach
the tenement stairway. (What?
I must be happy!)

36.
If I should die here
behind this bed, what a farce
it shall all have been!

[A bizarre misreading. The second
line should properly run: *on these
worn stairs, what a joy.* There
can surely be no real excuse for
such culpably cakeless mistakes!]

37.
"It's a farce! A farce!
A total farce!" (Yes? And yet –
what else could it be?)

[*Spurious.*]
[I am no longer quite so sure.]

38.
"Progress. Yes. Then what?
Perhaps more progress. Yes. Are
we there yet? Now what?"

39.
("I heard him say he
had glimpsed the final vision
and died of sameness.")

[Terminal delirium, no doubt.]

40.
"Maybe not," she said.
"But identity is quite
another matter."

41.
Change after change – and
yet – pretty much the same tears
they started out with…

[No. Too far-fetched.]

42.
"If only I had
not missed that flight, perhaps I'd
be immortal now!"

43.
Keep out of those woods,
Mr Dante! Little good
will come of such jaunts.

44.
(Who could have guessed that
the afterlife would be quite
so Italian?)

45.
"I thought I was sure
to live forever – and, as
it turns out, I *did!*"

46.
How sinuously
those long insects crept out of
the dead saint's nostrils...

47.
The Universe is
in both main senses a sort
of plant, is it not?

48.
"I had not the first
notion how to get back here
at this time of night!"

49.
Two seagulls strutting
through a school playground in the
summer holidays…

50.
Three late butterflies
landed on the great walls and
caused them to collapse.

51.
("A gifted sniper
could pick any of us off
at any moment.")

52.
When the song ended,
not a few of the houseflies
fell from the ceiling.

[Probably a slight improvement on the original – but not by
much.]

53.
"I've been swatting flies
with this same *Arts Section* for
quite a few days now!"

54.
Was that really a
bat which shot across the path
there not quite in sight?

(Something monosyllabic at any
rate.)

55.
No? What do you mean –
it's hard enough for a dream
to seem like a dream?

[Or *be*]

56.
The train hurtles past
a glade. Someone wearing red?
Or just, something red?

57.
And if I'm only
a fragment of your dreams, please
sleep on forever.

[Is there not also something to
be said for 'figment'?]

58.
(If only the whole
Universe had taken place
long before it [actually] did!)

[Or *after*, for that matter.]

59.
("How *dare* my parents
have existed for so long
prior to my birth!")

60.

There's something almost
poignant about Time as such
isn't there, Cronus?

61.

"What? Make a new world?
I'm sorry – but haven't I
done that already?"

62.

("Ultimate wisdom?
Hmm... Well... I'm not sure I can
quite recommend it.")

63.

(There's no way in which
I can honestly tell them
what they want to hear!)

64.

"Look. Just try to do
the most good you can – all right? –
and hope for the best."

[Replace *all right* with *said God?*]

65.

"It's just what I do –
since I had more or less no
chance to do much else."

66.
(The final problem
is simply what is the case
just as it all ends.)

67.
Is this real person
actually here? What more
is true enchantment?

68.
Drifting with such grace
through diaries scribbled down
centuries ago…

69.
Gasping on a bed –
neither for the first nor (with
luck) for the last time.

70.
A decayed old chair
listing out in the garden
for more than a year.

71.
"Oh, I'm pretty sure
my first wife must have cracked that –
though she said nothing."

72.
More clothes draped over
a rusting old telescope
out on the back lawn!

[Sky-blue? (Imaginatively d[r]ying out.)]

73.
High shoes. A straw hat.
Muse. What do you think of that?
Too bright for this sky.

74.
What landscape could give
quite so much to look at as
that veranda did?

75.
"Stay there on the grass!" –
said the other voice in a
neighbouring garden.

76.
Near noon. A child is
shouting "Please help me!" in a
school playground nearby.

77.
All this hidden life
unseen beyond even a
narrow empty lane!

78.
Why am I even
looking at an atlas now?
Are all these towns full?

79.
There where the roads meet –
they go to left or right – or
come from Left and Right.

80.
"I don't know. Naked
pregnant women? It's all too
deeply confusing."

81.
Checking the street-map
for the one square in which she
too must be right now...

82.
Ms glad they are Ms.
Ns glad they are Ns. And yet –
most lost, even so.

83.
By now we are all [vastly]
the late results of other
human impulses.

[Lose the loose word. And a final 'people's decisions' would
    surely be better?]

84.
"How cruel we are –
making sure only women
can have the children!"

85.
(And yet, for all that –
how one life-form keeps coming
out of another...)

86.

People climbing in
through their neighbours' windows rarely
spout as they do so.

[Ambiguous? An allegory?

(possibly sexual?)]

(Shout? Sport? Pout?)

[What isn't?]

87.

All those skeletons
making their way up and down
in so many lifts!

['down so many stairways' is
obviously preferable.]

88.

A loudspeaker in
the nearby church is saying
something or other.

89.

Near the holy shrine –
two fat clerics arguing
with a bus-driver.

90.

Pilgrims crowd the coach –
which soon leaves for the centre
of the universe.

91.
So many fleeting
holy places careering
through limitless space!

92.
This grain of sand here
in the universe is the
special talking one.

93.
"*Empty space* is a
contradiction in terms to
my way of thinking."

[*said the Lord?*]

94.
All these skeletons
carried along inside us –
aware of quite what?

[Indeed. Were we ever/even really introduced?]

95.
Distant sunlight from
the mirror in the hallway
almost finds us *here*.

[Two of my favourite words!]

96.
One thing surprised me
about the Sun last night. Yes.
But then – what *was* it?

[Obvious error for 'the Moon'.]

97.
No! I didn't want
this morning's sun to come out
at *quite* this moment.

98.
("Yes. It's something which
drifts about quite openly
in the public sky.")

[Not 'in the pub[l]ic sky'? Rather missed a trick there, Maxi,
    I would have thought.]

99.
"One thing surprised me
about your response last night – "
"Oh, that wasn't me!"

100.
The Moon sometimes shines
into this side-bedroom – but,
more often, doesn't.

101.
(What? I'm *here*, am I?
I'm not in the next room? No?
Well, well, well, well, well....)

102.

Moonlight on the wall –
right beside the picture of
a sunlit garden.

103.

I don't understand
how this half-lit world can be
quite so out of place.

104.

Through gaps and cracks, they
all watch snow falling onto
an endless blind plain.

[Hmm. If this isn't already a translation, it probably *ought* to
be.]

105.

An umbrella halts
for some reason, just behind
a dull, rain-lashed wall.

[Hyndland Road or thereabouts, by the sound of it?]

106.

A fly rebounding
off my head – merely one more
natural object.

107.

Bees buzzing here – and,
beyond some nearby walls, a
large crowd at prayer.

108.

("Surely in the past
they all knew each other? There
were so *few* of them!")

[Hello again.]
[Depending on who the 'they' are, this could even be true!]

109.

All these beetles! And
not a single one of them
knows it's not on Mars!

110.

("It took them too long
to grasp that the whole thing was
just meant to be *sung*.")

111.

The immense armies...
The millions of killers who
don't know each other...

112.

"From time to time, I
remember what it was like.
(I must have been mad!)"

[God is still speaking, I think?]
[Nonsense!]

113.
"Please (I prayed) let me
never find out what she has
let other men do!"

[An 'earnest cry and prayer' if ever there *was* one.]

[Slightly too late, by the sound of it.]

114.
"I do now regret
throwing all those old photos
into the Kelvin."

[Glasgow's most picturesque important river.]
['not'?]

115.
(I once found a snap
of someone's private parts in
a library book!)

[Not in the Archaeology section, I hope?]
[More probably, Local History.]
[Genealogy! (Always a popular subject.)]

116.
"Oh, we were both mad
back then, all the time!" laughed their
surviving parent.

117.
("My beloved son!
The result [alas] of a really
bizarre one-night stand...")

118.
"A character as
complex-delicate as an
archangel's first fart."

[A shameless plagiarism from
Cardenio, I would strongly suggest.]

119.
"Yes. Next to lying
to them – my worst mistake was
not lying to them."

[Another one!]

120.
(Yes. It all worked out
rather well in the end for
such a disaster.)

121.
How can so many
flightless golden birds end up
in this top-floor flat?

['Flightless' is clearly wrong. 'Sightless' perhaps, or is that not
    much better if at all? 'Golden' is barely adequate. But isn't
    something like 'gasping' not what we are really looking for
    here? *Shafts?*] Waht?.

122.
(Yes. While most of us
is looking for something which
isn't really there!)

123.
What is that leaking out
of those high windows up there?
(Silent joy, perhaps?)

124.
Ah, yes. Lost feathers.
What are the dreams which make them
fix regrets like that?

[Quills? Hopelessly obscure. Possibly pornographic?]

125.
"Copy the entire
universe – then take good care
not to misplace it!"

[Is this God again? [[*What a title!*]] Or *another* god?]

['displace it' would be even better, would it not?]
[Or at least as good. Not that either would actually be
    possible, I freely admit!!]

126.
And yet – who could such
a suggestion possibly
be being aimed at?

127.
Is there such a thing
as indeterministic
materialism[, darling]?

[Yes, of course there is.

With sufficient complexity.

Emergence *etcetera*.

Chaotic instability. Fluttering wings

I'm a bit of a Maxwell myself in fact!]

128.
"But how do we know
that the Cosmos as such is
not another one?"

[Ah, yes. The great questions!

(Theology. So much Philosophy.)

Not to mention, innumerable [*other?*]
types of mental aberration.]

129.
(Somewhere or other
a phone ringing as we walk
through the small churchyard.)

130.
How do I know that
I'm *really* sitting on my
backside, for instance?

[Why not italicise *my* as well?]

131.
("Of course the whole thing
must be real. Am I as tall
as I ought to be?")

132.
"Life is transient
only in the sense that it
won't last forever."

[Enough is enough! Who is this person?]
[Who is this person?]

133.
"But surely that which
lasts forever cannot quite
be so important?"

[So unimportant.]

134.
Just another grave
up on the slope – but this time
we stop beside it.

135.
May we be quite sure
that the Cosmos as a whole
isn't somewhere else?

[Haven't we already had this one?]
[No doubt a weaker early version, accidentally retained.]
[Perhaps much like the Cosmos itself?]

136,

[Alas, No. 136 is very probably a little too politically divisive
to be included here.]

137.

Then our bus appears –
round the sharp corner from where
ever it had been!

[The slightly unorthodox line-break here does at least seem
to (as it were) give a nod in the direction of the sudden ar-
rival of a perhaps not altogether reliable medium of public
transport.]
[(Not to mention the sudden change of subject?)]

138.

"Nobody *ever*
gets on at this bus-stop here!
(What's their little game?)"

139.

So many bus-stops
with only a single life
waiting there. (Or none.)

140.

So many bus-stops
where only one person is
waiting. (Still waiting.)

141.

Such a range of soles
walking smartly each day past
the Mortuary.

[By 'range', he – if it *is* a he – no doubt means 'variety' (the better word by far). The pun, though serious, is nonetheless accidental.]

142.
Students from all ends
of the earth, held back by the
Byres Road traffic lights!

143.
So many beauties
come somehow from the [Far] East to
these humdrum buildings…

144.
That old hospital [near us]
where so many must have
        died [by now]
has been demolished [at last!].

[Hardly a triumph of the form.]

145.
My God! It seems our
contemporaries really
do die after all…

146.
Trying a shortcut
through the cemetery, we
slow down anyway.

147.
Oh! An ambulance
parked outside a betting-shop!
Yes. Well... Best of luck...

148.
Not even nowhere
now doing nothing – as if
that needs to be stressed.

149.
These damned flies! No. They
can't *all* be emissaries
of the dead, can they?

150.
Just about to sneeze...
Perhaps in some ways what God
feels like all the time?

151.
Hard not to sense an
intended insult in all
this endless *throbbing*.

152.
Who is to blame for
all this – given that it can't
possibly be [Ze]us?

153.
Some people tell me
I remind them of God quite
a bit... Flatterers...

154.
("Is it *my* fault if
I'm superior to all
I see around me?")

155.
"Then I realised:
'*What? No. Wait* – I'm *Almighty
God! Yes* – Me! *What* Fun*!*'"

156.
Nor do I think much
of that obscure presence which
confuses us all.

157.
After yet one more
ordinary day at work,
I, er – excuse me –

[(I dare say one has to maintain a certain defensive inde-
terminacy around the edges, is that it? Since, otherwise,
people will almost exactly see what is going on – and
might well be disheartened by the sorry clarity of its lim-
itations?)] [No?]

158.
"What a great age it's
possible to reach – yet still
know next to nothing!"

159.
(I seem to have lived
my whole life by mistake. Can
that be possible?)

160.
"If all delusion
fell out of our lives, no-one
would live a full day."

161.
Truly, Man is the
delusional animal –
even *me* sometimes.

[A direct plagiarism from Aristotle, if I remember rightly.]

162.
Imagine having
to share a universe with
snakes[, stars] and psychopaths…

[In certain moods and moments, one feels that almost
    anything might serve as an appropriate final line here (and
    with many a personal name indeed among them!) – pro-
    vided it could be manoeuvered into the statutory cluster of
    syllables.]

[Just like the above?]

163.
"At last – an end to
our useless lifelong attempts
to get it all right!"

[Not quite. (Wouldn't 'hopeless' be better?)]

164.
(What complex project
does anyone ever get
absolutely right?)

165.
And if the whole world
should collapse forever – well…
that's just what it did.

[Wrong tenses, surely?]

166.
Having seen all there
is to see, my gaze reverts
to an extinct star.

[Unoriginal. (Except perhaps in its untruthfulness.)]

167.
'The same name here points
to three quite different men
who did not exist.'

[It may perhaps be worth pointing out that, in its original
    incarnation, the previous pair of examples referred to more
    than one extinct star?]

168.
How different is
one non-existent Being
from another? Yes?

169.

"To bring more people
to life"? Well – yes. But, from *where*?
Where they were before?

[Before they existed *at all*, presumably.]

170.

(The Source is silent
on the reasons for more or
less everything.)

171.

Intense scrutiny
from the cats, as they watch us
hanging a picture.

172.

[What do our p[o]ets think
is going on?] [By the way –
what *is* going on?]

173.

As if the past too
was not often also packed
with crowds and strangers!

[No. I wouldn't bother comparing this with No. 108 myself.]

174.

What? Are all these dots
real people? Dots all the way
to the horizon?

[Old photographs, perhaps?]

175.
Treat me equally –
(perhaps by giving me your
special attention?)

176.
Two schoolboys pausing
for a moment at a case
of new-found fossils.

[Or schoolgirls.]

177.
(Don't think of a moose.
(Have you done that? Good. (And now,
don't think of a mouse.)))

178.
"No. I was trying
just then to think about our
entire history."

179.
Sitting in a bright
kitchen, reading about how
old stars will die out.

180.
Checking the names of
Saturn's moons while waiting for
the kettle to boil.

181.
Left lying on the
microwave, a book about
the world of the Picts.

182.
[Unfortunately, No. 182 was so all-surpassingly wise, it would
have quite unbalanced the present work.]

183.
"This too is derived
from something else, I take it?"
"Well – yes. It *must* be."

[They can't *both* be God?]

184.
These early morning
wrenchings-apart are unknown
to our elements.

[Personally, I prefer molecules.]

185.
("How can I have made
exactly the same mistake
as all the halfwits [did]?")

186.
"Yes – this is still me,"
she said into the phone, with
Godlike nonchalance.

[Godlike. Stellar. Sublime. *Choose!*]

187.
"I've already had
enough dream-like drama for
one lifetime, thank you."

188.
("Hmm, yes… More of an
[emotional] education than I might
really have wanted [or needed]!" [, said the Lord.])

[*Consummatum est*, eh? Or what?]

189.
All sorts of output
may quite reasonably be
addressed as 'darling'.

[details / seriously]

190.
(The word 'man' needs one
syllable. The word 'woman'
requires two of them.)

191.
"If there are only
two spaces left, say 'Chinese'.
If three, 'Japanese'."

[How all the empires appear and disappear! Time for anoth-
er change, I fancy.]

192.
This awkward starlight
of hearing you disagree
with somebody else!

[Something has indeed gone wrong here. *Importantly*
   wrong.]

193.
"Yes. That's almost the
very point I was trying
to hint at myself."

194.
(Nothing is something
else. Nor are these animals
not just what they are.)

[Eh? What animals are these?]

195.
"Everything is
not what it isn't. (And then
some!) Yes. (Then some more!)"

196.
(What might I [not] have done
without all those [other] people who
never existed?)

[No, no, no. What might all these
other people who never existed
have done with *us*?]
[Or, indeed, *without* us?]

197.
Only the fates of
the people we are not quite
makes us hesitate.

[Corrupt. Make, obviously. Or perhaps fate. But I suspect
this should really be faith anyway. Or, of course, faiths.
('Faces' is, alas, impossible.)]

198.
Such divine flickers
veering away in the mind
before they're quite caught.

['diverse'? Of course, in the end, there is really no such thing
as 'at the exact same moment', is there?]

199.
These depthless visions –
which appear and disappear
at the [exact] same moment!

200.
Must this be your world?
(Turn the mirror round! (Have I
turned it round too far?))

[Perhaps not quite far enough.]

201.
So deep a failure
it ultimately became
a triumph of sorts...

202.
A long-odds-against
apparition – with real lives
and real deaths in it.

203.
(Even if they had
triumphed above all belief,
they'd still be dead now.)

[Slightly ignoble, if I'm not mistaken.]

204.
Yes. There's only so
much the entire universe
can do, isn't there?

205.
And compared to what
else is the All quite such a
matchless masterpiece?

206.
"It all seems to flout
our human sense of scale – but –
where else can we go?"

[Where do we come from? The simplest facts of human
    biology themselves flout the human sense of scale.]

207.
Intelligible?
Why should it be? Nothing has
left the scale unmarked.

208.
Mere routine shakes off
one impossibility
after another.

209.
"No. You cannot grasp
even the full scale of your
insignificance."

[Evidently the end of the affair!]

210.
("On the other hand:
were it not for Death, what would
they all talk about?")

[Really? Not 'Life' and 'we'?]
[Perhaps better cut out the three lines or so down to 'so
    insignificant that even this insignificance is insignificant'?
    yes. now utterly superfluous.]

211.
"The final moment
is *so* important – if we
ever notice it."

212.
"What I think we ought
to bear in mind," I said – but
she'd just left the room.

213.
After two hours of
expert lovemaking (alas)
he became three flies.

[Have we not had these flies before?]

[There are too many flies in this work.]

[Line 3 must read 'they'.]

[Surely 'two' and 'three' are the wrong way around here?]

[After two *years*?]

[Keep it real. Only a single fly. Too like Kafka.]

[Who?]

214.
How the eyes are drawn
inexorably towards
their shyest detours!

[I have almost said enough.]

215.
Something fell down from
one of the trees near us and
seemed to hurry off.

216.
Such a strange effect –
all those dots falling! But what
does it matter now?

[Stars?]

217.

What then? Death. Dust. Space.
Darkness. And one more planet –
eventually?

218.

Did we really live [together]
for all those days, so many
million years ago?

219.

A harsh wind blowing [here]
for many millions of years
totally unchecked.

[Why has the last line been changed from 'but never no-
ticed'?]
[Bit of a misjudgement, surely?]

220.

The Moon is the Moon.
And, in not quite the same place,
the Earth is the Earth.

[Or 'the Earth's something else.']

221.

How can they have missed
making it an offence to
be as old as this?

[Or, perhaps more simply, *feel.*]

222.
For something which does
not exist, the Past has a
strange self confidence.

[An oddly sharp memory, I would say.]
[Intermittently, at least.]

223.
All that urgent talk
in so many shielded rooms
down the scored-out years!

224.
A garden. A lane.
Whispers. (A plan that went wrong.)
A door slamming shut?

[Nice try!]

225.
A large rock thudding
into the ocean. Huge waves...
Then... some smaller waves...

226.
(There is just too much
Nature happening wildly
all over the place.)

227.
The sea again! No.
There's just too much of it. Why
are we not all drowned?

228.
That's nearly always
how it starts. is it not? No?
From the depths of space…

229.
A midget penis
rising briefly out of a
limitless ocean.

[Presumably allegory rather than straightforward reportage.]

230.
A calm, gilt figure
seated enthroned for years near
the bathroom window.

[Evidently some kind of religious image.]

[What? In their bathroom?]

231.
"No. They can never
be a God, a demon, a
woman, or a ghost."

[Hmm. These roles *very nearly* all have non-existence in
common, don't they?]

232.
Releasing a fart –
just as bells start to ring out
from a nearby church.

[Something of a study in sonorities, I suppose.]
[The satire inherent in mere reality.]
[Which is the more natural phenomenon?]

233.
Once again, the song
Happy Birthday ripples out
from the nearby school.

234.
Someone's child – almost
every morning – being
rushed into school – late!

235.
"My niece now goes to
a school which I've never seen.
In this same city!"

236.
("Is that guy up there
opposite the school, fixing
a car-door, or what?"

237.
This sudden [lively] child here –
suddenly fifty-eight years
younger than myself.

238.
(Along the next path,
a window among the trees.
Someone *behind* it!)

[Replace with: 'Someone *moving* there!'?]

239.
So many beings
battering at the windows
to get in or out...

240.
(On other planets
too – do you think they sometimes
can't stand each other?)

[That's *us*, is it not?]
[do you sometimes think they]

241.
"You don't mind if I
behave in a mental way
with your life, do you?"

[One could surely produce an entire lengthy book (not to say
    the full *oeuvre* of a rich and active life) simply by ringing
    the changes on *mental* and *life* – the ninth and thirteenth
    words here?]
[Oh why bother! Just program a machine to do it.]
[Menial?]

242.
So many females
saying "No!" (or, indeed, "Yes!")
at just this moment.

[Wrong way round?]
[*people* would be better]
[Again, the last four words of line 2 could reasonably admit
    innumerable adventures, and alternatives.]

243.
Then all go off in
different directions for
different reasons.

[Though similar reasons would surely do just as well?]

244.
But what do we know
of what makes us what we are –
not even ourselves.

245.
All kinds of rare stuff
going on in here somewhere.
Yes… Too much, perhaps?

246.
[Most regrettably, No. 246 was also felt to be too revealing to
be included.]

247.
A range of hills. Roofs.
Moonlight. Promising footsteps.
A steady downpour.

248.
Always so many
vultures arriving, whether
we watch them or not.

249.
Up there! One more jet
that we're not flying in! (Hmm…
Two of them in fact.)

250.
The crass insult of
all these exquisite face[t]s –
glimpsed once and then gone!

251.
Night. Who else might be
looking down at this side-street
as her car drives off?

252.
The next door along.
And then the one after that.
And then what? Ourselves?

253.
["Yes. It's probably
more Loave Street, Glasgow,
than anywhere else."]

[I feel it is hardly necessary to point out that there is in fact
    no such place. (Certainly I have never been able to find any
    such address myself – and, believe me, I have searched for
    it long and hard.)]

254.
[Sadly, just that bit *too* difficult to merit retention.]

255.
Morning. Look! The street
is *again* full of people
going off to work.

256.
"I'm simply full of
admiration for them. Full
of admiration."

257.
Thus, day after day,
they disappear – (then come back!) –
and what do *I* do?

258.
(In rare high pulses
we dream we have glimpsed how much
there is to it all.)

259.
Morning. Who else might
be looking down at this street
as these cars drive off?

260.
(Yes. I'm the right twin.
Which means I am more or less
sacred, does it not?)

261.
"Why can't Truth as such
take her ill-fitting clothes off
a bit less sadly?"

[Or, in certain moods, 'more quickly'.]

262.
Try to stay like that
for as long as you can. What?
No... You've moved slightly.

263.
By all means sit down
on that new cushion with the
clouds printed on it.

[Rather than the one which has the *Tyrannosaurus* on it.]

264.
(All day, this park bench
receives one pensive buttock
after another.)

[Can this be quite right?]

265.
The cat sits staring
at nothing while the music
sweeps this way and that.

[Was it *Coppélia* that evening?]

266.
If there were only
music which reminded me
of her dancing face!

[? If only there were…]

[*dreaming* surely]

267
"Something happened there!"
screamed the Creator. "There! Just
then! What was that? Eh?"

268.

(In fact [*said the angel*], the Lord does
not bother his [sublime] arse about
merely 'real' objects.)

269.

What was that weird noise?
Something has happened downstairs
by the sound of it.

270.

Do please excuse us
while we sit here weeping. [Or,
by all means, join in.]

271.

Up among the stars –
people trying to clean new
arrivals' backsides.

272.

"I'm not sure. Are there
no lavatories *at all*
in the Vatican?"

FGJPQY

273.

Which of them don't? All
these great public figures, priests,
leaders, mystics, saints…

[I think he's claiming that they all need[ed] to shit.]

274.
Or shall our children
(at long last!) be the ones who
do not have to die?

275.
Though, for them, the end
of the world seems to happen
more or less each day…

276.
("No-one – not even
God's own Ma – has ever raised
a child properly.")

[Certainly it's odd, to say the least,
that we should happen to have been
told the name of Almighty God's grandmother.]

277.
'From near the outputs
of our excrement, why should
Gods too not emerge?'

[Onestone?]

278.
(Hurrying off for
a shit, still humming the Bach
Et Incarnatus!)

279.
Hurrying away –
a figure from years ago –
with a child in tow!

280.
Vast crowds of pilgrims
are something else which gases
could expand into.

281.
So what if it is
possible even to kill
someone politely?

282.
"Please stop doing that!"
screamed a voice across the lane.
(Hmm. Such an odd *please*.)

283.
(You know, for a mere
cul-de-sac, this place can be
strangely eventful...)

[Astronomy again?]

284.
Joy – hard words – silence –
all shall alike revert to
gases, shall it not?

[Or – perhaps not *exactly* gases.]

285.
All 'those things' we said –
precious moves – a swirling mist
millions of years off.

286.
What a reaction!
I move a complex hand back
to where it came from.

287.
That was freedom or
life ending right here, was it?
(No? Then, what *was* it?)

288.
"I don't know where it
is – unless [perhaps] I left it in
my other domain."

289.
Incoherent cries
going on in all the rooms
of the same building...

290.
"I didn't expect
quite so many moths to fly
out of these trousers!"

291.
(Has it [really] come to this?
Falling over while pulling
off my underpants?)

292.
Look! It's one more great
spiritual leader with
poor bladder control...

293.
("'*Pope Calls For Peace In
Violent World*'. And – you know –
I *agree* with him!")

294.
Are none of these vast
worshipping crowds fighting the
urge to have a blast?

295.
'No. Not I who fart,'
thinks the mystic. 'But, rather,
God who farts through me.'

296.
("Truly, that was a
humblingly profound motion
of airwaves, Master.")

[profoundly humbling?]

297.
"I'd never undressed
among such spiritual
prodigies before!"

298.
Which of them are so
sheltered that they can't also
use a shutter too?

[Hopelessly corrupt.]

299.
("This is the first day
I have been stark-naked since
I arrived on Earth!")

300.
Struggling for value
in words and deeds, before we
dissolve forever.

301.
[Too obscene.]

302.
("Is this wiping-out
of helpful lives not the shame
of the universe[, Lord]?")

303.
No. The All does not
even hear our music – far
less dance to our tune.

304.
Future extinction[s]
moving around us with such
finesse on all sides!

305.
Yes. Endless shame on
the world for coming into
existence at all...

306.
("And yet – how can it
be reasonable to blame
nothingness as such?")

307.
Perhaps even a
point when these last damned insects
will have vanished too?

308.
(All real afterlives
as such are at best merely
metaphorical [said the Lord].)

[And how does anyone know this?]
[The same way anyone can know anything, I suppose, if it's
    true.]
[Yes, yes. But how do we know whether it's true or not in the
    first place?]
[It seems to me I have just answered that very question. Have
    I not?]
[Who are these bloody people

309.
[Technically libellous. Better remove.]

310.
Millions of years since
any frog last jumped into
or out of this pond.

[Consider: 'till', 'will jump into or out of', 'thousands', 'toads'.]
[The pond is *still here*?]

311.
Slowly, the huge shim
sinks below the surface of
the resettling sea.

[Presumably the obvious misprint – rather than the second
most obvious one – although the given word certainly
exists. (Shim: a type of washer.)]
[All those 's's! All that bubbling and gurgling!]
[Just thought I'd point that out.]

312.
Pulses of light rain
falling forever on roofs
attached to nothing…

[Nonsense as it stands.]
['attracting'?]
[comma after *roofs*]

313.
A limitless sea –
with so many capsized lives
drifting to and fro

[Yes, yes. But the simpler 'capsized boats' is probably still
more powerful for all that, is it not?]

314.
In this patch of light
something could be happening
to poise a whole world.

315.
"All [supposed] final meanings
are fantasies which they have
dreamed up for themselves."

[Is this who I think it is?]
[Is it ever?]
[Well, is *this* who I think it is?]

316.
(If the *Source Of All
That Is* is not [also] the source of
evil, then what is?)

317.
It's beyond belief
what gets left at the top of
this Sacred Mountain!

318.
All else less needed
than that head on the pillow
for another hour.

319.
Which of us have not
shipped away many a time
into nothingness?
[misprint for 'slipped']
[Just get rid of it.]

320.
Then we all wake up
into something or other
which seems to matter [more].

[*Seems*, Madam?
Nay, tell me what *does matter* more.]
[More than dreams, presumably.]

321.
Heat! Suddenly so
many instincts all around
us, aware of what?

[insects!]

322.
What was I thinking
about just then? Sighs. Size. Thighs.
Ah, yes! Chlorophyll…

323.
(No-one will ever
know what I'm looking at as
I scribble this down!)

[He thinks he's God too!]

324.
A mere blade of grass
has managed to develop
such vast self-conceit.

["I come ever closer by the day to considering that all of us
    have something which matters more to us than does mere
    limping Reality itself." (*Hos Re*)]

325.
"Why not put your faith
in stuff which is *there*? Or is
that just too naïve?"

[Or *painful*?]
[How much faith does the self-evident require?]

326.
Between one's first breath
and one's last, one often needs
to do many things.

[It needed no Ghost, my Lord, come from the grave to tell us
    that!]
[Isn't *to do one more thing* better?]
[START HERE]

327.
("After you have thought,
'I'm ready to die now!' – life
flourishes again.")

328.
"After death, I grew
less and less ashamed of my
humble origins."

[So. Not quite in Paradise yet!]

329.
("I wish I were dead!
Oh, no – wait a minute. I
am dead, am I not?)

(Ah! How many of us can honestly
make that proud boast?)

[Another one!]

330.
"Oh, they *adore* me –
till they find out who I [really] am…
(Which they never [quite] do.)"

331.
"No. I didn't have
much luck with not being me.
And now it's too late…"

332.
"My real mistake, I
now think, was letting my spouse
find out how I am."

[Before I even knew myself?]
[Well… for that matter…]
[Some infelicities are just so difficult to avoid, aren't they?]
[misprink for 'who'.]

333.
"Don't go looking for
a perfect mate round here, Mate –
that's *so* immature."

334.
[Sadly, it has proved
to be necessary to
do without this one.]

[Thank you. Such exquisite tact.]
[The World shudders and goes on.]

335.
[Damn!] And I lack space here
for my [irrefutable] proof that it's better
to be good than bad!

[Format!]
[Fermat?]

336.
(Saving somebody
else's life was almost the
last mistake [s]he made!)

337.
"How could the All be
an honest advertisement
for a More-Than-All?"

338.
The new-born babe stretched
out its arms and asked: *What is
the point of it all?*

339.
This sublime quest for
a profounder realm beyond
the deepest real one!

[*For* sublime *read* absurd?]

340.
"Personally, I
suspect there is [really] no such thing
as the speed of light."

341.
How pointless it would
be – but for the living fling
of the pointlessness [itself]!

342.
All these fine bones, now
heaped together here, after
lives both good and bad…

[Anywhere?]

343.
These old bones perhaps
once sustained a fine grasp of
classical Latin.

344.
Someone else shouting
desperately for help in
a long-dead language!

345.
"Yes, Madam. Truly,
a transcendent cult-centre,
if I may say so."

[Yes. That's exactly the sort of thing he *would* have said!]

346.
Hundreds of old, used
rail tickets in a box in
the dead wife's bedroom.

347.
A lost (still valid)
train-ticket lying at the
Hospital Entrance...

348.
Night. The train mistakes
this next station for a real
place – and stops there too.

349.
(Yet again, the urge
to get out here and [somehow] start a
new and better life...)

350.
I missed the last train!
Otherwise I'd not now be
sitting on this bed.

351.
"Isn't it simple?
We observe a lot, and then
we cease to exist."

352.
What's that line down there?
A river? A road? A wall?
Or just some fluked *line?*

353.
"Few paths are quite as
precarious as the ones
in one's underwear."

354.
How many billions
of miscarriages have there
been by now? (These crowds!)

355.
All those millions of
unique lives which lasted for
a few seconds each...

356.
Onto the bridges
from all directions, only
to disperse quickly.

357.
[Obviously far too inflammatory.]

358.
(From nothingness to
nothingness is not really
a journey, is it?)

359.
[Deplorable! Cut. Holy Grail of the Stale Pale Male or WHAT.]

360.
My sister-in-law –
(or, just possibly, my wife) –
is laughing upstairs.

[In fact, there was no such woman. (Or, indeed, *were*. Which
   is probably just as well – given that there was really no
   'upstairs' involved either.)]
[Such quite unnecessary evasiveness!]
[On the other hand, at least the laughter was real enough, I
   suppose.]
[(By far the most important thing!)]

361.
I keep confusing
the words in her language for
paths, morning and *love.*

362.
"I like to buy them
flowers, since I like to hear
them talk about them!"

[I don't know. Perhaps something of a study in sheer ugliness
   of expression?]

363.
This bauble bought from
a street-stall will soon be put
to a thrilling use!

364.
"Some have wee wans an
others prefer big wans an
that's that but. So what?"

[A hint here of a charming local dialect?]

365.
"That's not the right one!"
said the Archangel, looking
utterly confused.

366.
Alas, I could not
quite get in through the only
viable window.

367.
(Oh there are *always*
some things to be pulled up and
others to pull down!)

368.
"Really, I think what
we need to try to do here
is pull them sideways?"

[Such a typically witty suggestion!]

369.
(A predictable
yet extraordinary
development. Yes.)

370.
"It looks too blunt. Art
thou quite sure this equipment
is up to the job?"

371.
"Oh! This size *at least*!"
said the doctor, waving her
cultured hands about.

372.
"This lacks any for
much the same reason that that
other one didn't."

373.
"I would have preferred
a goddess." ("Wouldn't we all?")
"*Much* more natural."

["Much more *natural*," surely?]

374.
I still can't quite seem
to get out through the only
actual window.

375.
"But no doubt we're not
meant for this sort of merely
real world – are we, dear?"

376.
(No. *This* world is of
sufficient interest to
be getting on with.

377.
"So much so that words
like 'supernatural' must
be superfluous.")

378.
How could there not be
such unfathomable holes
at the heart of life?

[Too lowering. Change to "wholes" without comment?]

379.
(What? A mere *thing*? Some
sort of *mammal*, in fact? No.
It's just *not enough*!)

380.
"More mere sounding words.
'Immateriality'?
There is no such *thing*!"

[Hasn't there been rather too much of this by now?]

381.
And rank extinction
is the staying future of
whoever we like?

[Wouldn't 'love' be better? And 'straying'?]
['Love' no doubt. But here 'staying' evidently = inexorable,
    unavoidable. Sorry, but such it is. (Another Shakespearean
    usage.)]

[Not quite!]

382.
(For who can suppose
that there might be degrees of
absolute absence?)

383.

"Those Picts who worshipped
cracks were at least fixing on
something that exists!"

384.

If only the whole
World could be even more like
the one one worships...

[An anticipatory slip of some sort?]

385.

These lists of the dead!
More absolutely absent
whether loved or not.

[Just leave it all without any further clarification. I well
    remember his once saying to me: "The sad fact is, I don't
    actually want people to be able to work out every last
    detail."]

[As if anyone ever could!]

[Yes. Sometimes omniscience can be
just so limiting, can't it?]

[Passing off the outcome of an inability to capture something
    fully as if it were the end result of a deliberate policy of
    evasiveness!]

386.

"At least I had a
damn good laugh when I read his
obituary."

387.
("We were having a
damn good laugh – till it fell down
the back of the bed.")

388.
Going to bed late –
accompanied by oddly
helpful absences.

389.
"Why does my shadow
no longer do *exactly*
what I am doing?"

390.
Look how many leaves
are drifting – even though there
seems to be no breeze!

391.
That's my own shadow
flickering through the shadows
of this wood, is it?

392.
The 'thing' that sped off
is presumably still in
the garden somewhere?

393.
Across the back lane
(thud) all morning *(thud)* the same
relentless harsh dull –

394.
Many things must be
moving in the grass, even
during this still dawn.

395.
That rusted bucket
has been lying on its side
over there for years.

396.
What garden is not
utterly crawling with them
long after sunset?

397.
A dark river-town.
And there, among the dim roofs,
stairs and stairs and sta[i]rs!

398.
[Overtly obscune.]

399.
Dost walls crash down late
leaves fall mark a [f]lush last too
t'all (Ooo(h) Christ!) fates p[l]ush?

[Ah! Thank God for some genuine poetry at last...]

400.
So many waves have
lapped against these walls since last
I walked here, thinking –

[walked, stood, sat]

401.
Well: It's a small world
if one is the Atlantic
Ocean, I suppose.

402.
So many wrecked ships
buried somewhere beneath this
gently shaking sea!

[or *smoking?*]

403.
"Human history [all in all]
has about as much weight as
a fossilised sponge."

404.
("What was that he said?
'The acne of History'?
Oh – the *acme*"! Right…")

405.
He smiled, flapped his arms –
and began to rise smoothly
up through the Gray Sky.

406.
A strange bird landing
in our back garden, rather
than anywhere else...

407.
"Time is like a fly.
Yes. Well... not quite like that. But –
like its *wings* at least."

408.
Time is not much like
anything else – (said the Lord) –
including itself.

409.
("Hmm. Or might it be
that some things are *even more*
pointless than others?")

410.
"Oh, God – No!" screamed the
parrot. "I'm going to die
right now! And *for what?*"

411.
The toad's tongue erupts
from its resting-place – and now
one more life is not.

[Is it really a *toad* that does this?]
[Chameleons, I think?]

105

412.
"After killing some
stray callers, I found the night
dragging a little."

413.
The chameleon's
lightning tongue erupts – and one
more life vanishes!

414.
On the whole, I am
content that beetles cannot
talk about their lives.

[Or indeed their wives.]

415.
Help! I dreamt a flea
bit me – and woke to find I
had just been divorced!

[Yet another translation?]

416.
In a dream, two girls
claimed to come from a street which
I knew very well.

417.
An uncanny blur
moving about in a dim
room across the street –

[Worrying?]

418.
I don't know how to
interpret the eerie sounds
I can hear next door.

[Yes, yes. Does one ever quite?]

419.
From the next flat down –
the sudden anguished cry of
"My God! What a cunt!"

420.
("There was something of
the fairy-tale about, say,
ten weeks of my life.")

421.
Years now, since I saw
two girls leaving the house through
that corner window.

422.
"I think there may be
some suggestion that she turned
into a garden."

423.
On the country road
something the size of a head
lifts up from the mud.

424.
Two dried-out turds are
all that survive of a great
struggle in this shrine.

425.
Out weeding, while some
neighbouring TV broadcasts
a Royal Wedding.

426.
It killed more than one –
but now it helps a widow
with her gardening.

427.
Though autumn was still
far away, dead leaves covered
the earth this morning.

[Earth?]

428.
When I recall what
happened here last year, I thank
God for hidden doors.

[An angel is speaking, right?]
[Oh, so much of it is mere phenomenal mystification!]
[What? The Universe itself?]
[No. It went of its own accord.]
[How absolutely typical!]

429.
God, how tedious
these sta[i]rs are! So tedious.
All too tedious...

430.
The dark of the sea
squirms away, till it is now
the dark of the sky.

431.
"[Yes.] They were still waiting
for their real lives to begin
when old age coshed them."

[To beg in, eh?]

432.
(Hard to have to leave
too soon a planet still full
of what I can't name.)

[Actually, Eva, I suspect it has been named already.]

433.
"Oh, indeed! My words
are never quite the right ones.
... I've often said that."

434.
Next morning, we both
feared that the End of the World
might be overdue.

435.
Too many angels
are running over our roots
for total comfort.

[Surely 'roofs', even if the wrong ones! Perhaps they have
been confused with (or by) No. 312?]

436.
How could we two die?
Look how big the new table
in our kitchen is!

437.
"Perhaps it simply
doesn't quite realise that
it's inanimate?"

[What? The table?]
[Surely the Universe as such?]
[Oh for Heaven's sake! It was a *joke!*]
[What? The Universe as such?]
[No. What could the Inanimate ever actually 'realise' to any
extent at all?]
[Depends what we mean by 'realise', I suppose.]

438.
Fast, held in such tau[gh]t
golden chains, though so little
seemed to be offered –

[More or less meaningless?]
[Actually, not entirely devoid of profundity.]

[Both?]
[Neither.]
[More or less the same thing in the end!]

439.
"No. Nothing has gone
quite wrong here – though I don't know
what it is. Or not?"

[Indeed. If even such a dear and remarkable friend could die,
   then anyone can die.]
[Truly. And truly no-one is ever quite safe, however great or
   however convincing the occasional flattery may be.]

440.
"Two infernos – but
no-one is responsible
for either of them."

441.
("I had never screamed:
'The World's on fire! Get them off!'
to a chair before.")

[Self-evidently either a mere slip or incipient insanity.]
[Not so 'incipient' either!]
[a *choir?*]
[These days, people can be chairs too.]

442.
'Four rare antique fire
extinguishers were saved from
the blazing Town Hall.'

443.
"That's enough of that!"
the turd suddenly screamed in
the empty hallway.

[Oh, for God's sake! The *bird!*]
[Or 'the dodo'?] [Brilliant!]

444.
Enraged, he stormed out
of the flat, still carrying
a pair of knickers.

[God knows, it could so easily have been a whole lot worse ...]

445.
New Year's Day. Two men
carrying a large sofa
down the quiet street.

446.
A pair of brightly
coloured pants, curvetting through
the abandoned house!

[I suspect that these too are more probably allegorical than
    anything else.]
[A spiritual allegory?]

447.
"No. Whatever else
you do, please keep the feathers.
They're *such* a success!"

[A uniquely delightful effect.]

448.
How enviable –
not to be able to fall,
whatever happens.

449.
The angel she drew
is still there on the kitchen
table next morning.

450.
("It's hard to see birds
as being secondary
to anything else.")

451.
Who would have guessed it?
A Goddess without the least
sense of direction!

452.
"But I have *never*
called myself 'the greatest mind
of all time', have I?"

453.
Months passed, before a
wholly new technology
came to our rescue.

454.
[Self-pity. Semimental [?] Sentimental. Finnish here.]

455.
"Oh well – at least I
got to be *me*. A rare stroke
of luck that, surely?"

456.
(Ah, yes. How well one
knows the feelings! How well one
knows the feeling, yes…)

457.
No, I've never yet
met a "really great poet,"
Madam. Why – have you?

458.
They cast such fine nets
into the great wide ocean –
and draw out [next to] nothing!

459.
"No. Most of it's just
so much incantatory
fathomless bluffing."

460.
("Widely ignored as
a quite unignorable
artistic breakthrough…")

461.
"Still… Not even our
loudest farts blow any stars
out of their orbits."

[Just as well, I suppose.]
[Stars do orbit too, do they?]
[Yes. And so do stairs!]

462.
(Oh, it was nothing!
No. Merely our limitless
lives, loves and so forth.)

[Rather an all-purpose epitaph!]

463.
"And [my] heartfelt, if not
quite hundred percent sincere,
thanks to all of you!"

464.
"Still... we don't want to
take this whole existence thing
too seriously..."

465.
(No shortage of those
who have felt by now that life
goes on long enough!)

466.
But do, by all means,
tell me of some real thing more
important than this.

467.
"Looking back – I find
myself – wondering – what so
much loss turns into."

468.
(And no doubt many
have felt by now that their lives
went on for too long.)

469.
"We were *so clearly*
going to live for ever.
What happened to that?"

470.
(Yet, what we do and
what we don't do alike leave
it all as the All.)

[What about *feel?*]

471.
The greatest music
dissipates into the air
[much] like anything else.

472.
No, Love. There's no path
down which we shall meet again
after our deaths. None.

[Stark indeed, Angel – but is the truth too good for us? Or
    perhaps, not good enough? And what are we to do sooner
    than make the best of and out of any real world that we
    actually are, come what may, an intrinsic part of?
'For only this is where we only are.'
(Shakespeare, AWTE: 5.5.22)]

473.
(He wasn't real. So
they made him the Patron Saint
of non-existence.)

474.
"Of course, dying and
dissolving into thin air
is hardly *perfect*..."

475.
(Really, these days, all
I have to worry about
is – not dying *yet*.)

476.
"Well, I've had a go.
I [only] hope I didn't make a
complete mess of it."

477.
While we were waiting
for the test results, we talked
about her childhood.

[children?]

478.
So many doctors
hurrying through the building
with so much to do.

[Or 'city', I suppose.]
[*Too* much to do for that matter, eh?]

479.
How many of these
machines must people have been
wired up to by now –

480.
"It may feel as if
your eye is coming out. But,
don't worry. It won't!"

481.
"No. I feel too warm.
(I can't quite get used to it.
(Or am I too cold?))"

482.
(How near are we to
someone else who is thinking
'Can I be dying?')

[Or: Am I dying too?]

483.
"You know… I find this
process of dying not quite…
not *wholly* boring."

484.
("Right? What rights? We had
as much *right* to be here as
the dinosaurs did.")

['As little' is what he really means here, I think?]
[Or indeed do.]

485.

Perhaps it's time we
tried to get the whole thing done
all over again?

486.

No. These parasites
are as much what the whole thing's
about as we are [ourselves].

[True, no doubt. But could the first line here not just as legit-
imately invoke anything else whatsoever?]

487.

("I wasn't even
aware I was doing it!"
laughed the Creator.)

[Such a great pity that not a single one out of 'giggled', 'snig-
gered', 'chortled' or 'chuckled' is a monosyllable.]
[How about 'sneered'?]

488.

"One kindly old dog
dying is already too
much loss for a world."

489.

Now dog and cat [so loved] have
both been sidetracked off into
the same nothingness.

490.
Whether inside a
distant room or a nearby
head – is it the same?

491.
("Is that voice merely
a burst in my head – or a
limitless *something?*")

492.
The love that moves the
stars moves, say, crocodiles and
viruses as well.

[Virgintillions of them! And as many other such cases.]
[Why not mosquitoes too?]

493.
"Almost as if the
whole bright business were some sort
of mad forgery –"

[Of what *else?*]

494.
"[Well,] Of course the whole thing
can't really be reminding
me of something else!"

495.
Everything real
must fit into the real world
somehow or other.

496.
"No, I can't see how
there could be anything real
yet wholly elsewhere."

497.
[If "it" didn't, "it"
simply would not be here in
the first place, would it?]

498.
Is this world less like
a blurred sketch of our dreams than
of our private parts?

[One of the great Unanswerables!]
[Yes, well, is it even a real question, really?]

499.
Are we too naïve
or too knowing for this real
world? (Or, perhaps, both?)

[What else? *For what else?*]

500.
It's just what happens
when you stick your nose into
the Ultimate [W]Hole!

501.
Alas, there is just
no substitute for doing
the hard work, is there?

502.
While real delusions –
(though they exist in masses) –
remain delusions.

503.
"No 'Totality'
can reach beyond all this. There's
nothing else there. (Where?)"

504.
Everything real
has to be in a real place.
What place do you mean?

505.
(Fanciful gleams which
switch off and on for lifetimes
inside our real heads!)

506.
"Yes, well, the best thing
I can say about all that
is that it happened."

507.
(A fit epitaph
for the entire Cosmos, if
ever there was one!)

508.
In some modes, beyond
all praise – and, in others, all
out unbearable.

[Another near invisible misprint.]

509.
[And the worst would be,
that it hadn't happened? [Back
to the drawing-board!]]

510.
At l[e]ast no angels
posed nude for us, demanded
mere cash, and vanished.

[This almost sounds to me as if it has strayed in from another
    work entirely.]
(Maybe the next one?)
[*More* cash?]

511.
"To be quite honest,
I wasn't sure whether it
had ended or not!"

[Said the Almighty?]

512.
No doubt their atoms
are all still pulsing out there
somewhere or other.

513.
"We *still* don't have the
order quite right, do we? (If
there really is one.)"

514.
"Was that it? Something
else was already there in
place before the start?"

515.
("I wouldn't have missed
that for the whole world!") ("What? Was
that not what it was?")

516.
"I suspect even
Eternity might go by
extremely quickly."

517.
Of course they too will
never now realise that
they're inanimate!

518.
(Not the least untrue
Autobiography I've
flicked through for some time.)

519.
"Perhaps it's hopeless
for those who are expecting
too much from it all?"

520.
[How most of us were/
was looking for something which
wasn't really [t]here!]

521.
(One more fine day passed
in the warm glow of crowning
anticipation!)

522.
Was that one of our
perfect days? But it's gone now –
whatever it was...

NOT QUITE A FALSE FRESH START EITHER

1. NOT QUITE A FALSE FRESH START

Clocks were put forward an hour last night. So, on this clear bright morning,
I have the sloping, tree-lined city lane for once all to myself.
More slowly than ever, I walk down it an hour before I walk down it.

2. A CURIOUS INCIDENT ON A LATE SUMMER EVENING

I look out. Someone is strolling along the street towards the park.
Over there, someone else is gently walking a dog away from the park.
I had more or less decided to get up from this chair at the window.
Why should anyone want to wait, just to see two people walk past each
    other?

3. ANOTHER OF THESE PICTURESQUE LOCAL VIGNETTES

Okay. High time to get out there again –
for the day's messages, some fresh rolls, and (no doubt) another newspaper –

whatever was happening on this barely perceptible slope,
say, ninety-nine thousand years ago – although now

a charmingly girlish pair of (presumably) Chinese students
have stopped behind a strange obstruction of chairs left out in the street

to let this quaint old local, lost (it seems) in his own thoughts,
move more easily past them both, with almost no signal of thanks.

4. NO INSINUATION OF TENTACLES

Once again, I look up and glance out of the window just beside me.
Once again, there's only yet another wrong somebody else
walking unconcernedly down the street in this certainly more meaningful
    direction.
What's going on? Are only unknown people now allowed to come round
    that nearest corner?
Another sigh. I return to a startling book about the minds of octopuses.

5. A PRACTICAL DEMONSTRATION

What? Her key in the lock! (I hadn't even realised
she was out.) No. No – wait a minute. *Of course*
I knew she had gone out. Of course I did.
Dear God – can't any of these so-called great philosophers
ever get anything right? (Hello? No – I'm in here!)

6.

Children are once again pouring out of that school over there.
Dear me … Who can even think of all the schools there must be
on the planet. On all the planets. In this city. Raining still.
Will a few billion more years really be quite enough?
But – enough for what? Yes, that's the big question, isn't it?

7.

Across the road, a man unhurriedly opens the school gates.
First, the left-hand section. Good. Then, what we see as the right.
Morning again. Still pleasantly cool. And, yet again, the planet
has breath-takingly avoided splitting into two overnight.
Or even three. Or more. But two would surely have done it.

8. STILL WAITING

One more undistinguished planet somewhere among the millions of
    billions of stars.
It may not be as serious as we think it is.
No. All those different lengths of years passing on every last one of them!
But – it's very nearly noon. Yes. Surely the Hospital
would have phoned us by now if it really was something urgent?

9. VISITING TIME NOTES

The vast impressive frontage
of what I used to think

was chiefly a Children's Hospital
has at last been demolished

(surprisingly quickly at that) –

and, somehow strangely unlooked-for,
the old public clock-face

the hands of which had stood
static, stationary, motionless, fixed, rigid, unmoving
at five minutes to noon – (or, possibly, midnight) –

– (Yes – look! It really isn't moving!) –

that too must have gone
not quite patiently off
into some vague, shadowy, unpursuable
nowhere or other along with it – fit backdrop
for many a priceless local Eurydice.

(Don't worry about it. It should be all right.)

But – such a highly doubtful adornment
for any public building –
never mind a hospital!

(Unless perhaps its unique antique status had itself kept it safe till then?)

And it felt as if a rare resource
of continuing-continuous use and value
had been cruelly removed from us
before we had had even the most last-gasp chance
to seek out a second opinion –

once proverbially dead-right twice
on every single one of those days –

all those vital busy days
those difficult labouring days
all those routine annihilating days

(and what thanks do you ever get for it?)

Strange, to miss so livelily
(*"What did you bring those lilies for?"*)
what had by then long since become
so hardened, shameless and encrusted
a chronic habitual deceiver –

just because something vaguely internal
perhaps went wrong with a ratchet or lever?
(*All these arrivals! Yes. Then, all these leavers!*)

("Did you really *have* to talk so much about beavers?")

More than half a century –
and no-one (was it really no-one?)
had ever quite been able
(was it *really* half a century?)
to find enough time to fix it.

("I just can't find the time!")

("But – then again – who ever can?")

And, for that matter, did I ever give it
even a single passing-momentscaring
thought

on any one of the thousand or two occasions
when (fraught? relaxed? utterly ecstatic?)
I must have paced past within sight of it?

Well … perhaps I did.
I simply don't remember.
Always something else
going on unseen
behind the passing faces.

Like, say, this precarious visit
of what, if it were real,
one might even call hope

(and think how much hope, genuine hope,
must have arrived here… and then left)

that right there, near the very end,
not long before it went forever –
some fatal dislocation did

not jolt it back into life again:

nor some perfectly timed knock
during the fraught process
of ephemeral dismemberment

– (a mutilating strike
        mutating into
mock resuscitating progress) –

momentarily shocked it back
into a final spasm of action

("That corpse's arm moved, did it not?")

somehow stretching its hands beyond
mere real life and death –
now a parodic portent
of posthumous existence –

a face once more indicating
that all was still going on – still –
all of it – still –
(whatever this is) – going on –

perhaps even showing
a suddenly correct continuation

the minute that it actually was

exactly the right time of day
for whatever patched-up chaos
was continuing far below –

where at present a substantially new artery is being created out of the
    local road network.

10. IN THE MUSEUM OF MEDICAL CURIOSITIES

"Yes. I like to think
it must be the skull of an
extremely good, kind person –
Or an unusually
wise one, at the very least."

[One could almost think
all of human history
is a Museum
of well-dispensed medical
quirks and curiosities.]

11. TOGETHER

Later, we strolled down the gleaming Museum corridor
until we reached the glass case which displayed
the startlingly well-preserved footprints of one or two smallish dinosaurs.
Some twenty years since last I stood right here, just beside them.
Yes. That must have been me. Not alone that time either.

12. DOVER STREET

What, after all, are a few million active years
here and there among friends? And yet, is it not odd
that lives which were (of course) so specific cannot be
more specifically dated? Beings, say, like a fossil
which died a few hundred million years ago –
two or three, I suppose: Is that even a few? –
with an embryo still inside her, which would now
never develop into an evolving life of its own –

while, lingering on elsewhere in that same larger body,
were remnants of a third existence, suddenly
turned into thoughtless food, by one more strike
in an edgeless time packed out with strikes and misses –
as all things hit whatever they could do
with even less sense of acting prehistorically
that we ourselves have. The uncommitted minerals
retain from that unending cacophony
a few rings scattered here and there – and some of these
are now further processed for a far later discipline
of yet another life-form. Hence, for instance, the book
which I have set aside to come into this next room
and occupy the second chair that sits at the bay-window
where we too now have somehow arrived successfully together
after the giddying entanglements of so many unknown ancestors –
while, outside, another strangely normal evening begins to grow dark.
The first lights are being turned on at the windows across the street.
And still we know nothing (do we?) of who these people are
who are making all their purposeful decisions so near to us.

13. BRIGHT AND BEAUTIFUL

A gentle, beautiful, caring 21-year-old student
who loved animals – and who was soon to graduate
with a degree in Communication Studies
from a Jesuit College in California –
while on holiday in the Bahamas went off snorkelling
within sight of her loving parents – and was torn to shreds
(one arm severed, God knows what other injuries)
by a sudden group of, most probably, tiger sharks –
though since they quit the scene of their latest natural give-and-take
almost at once, this detail is not quite known for a certainty.

But off they went anyway, whatever they thought they'd been doing –
if anything of much substance – merely one more attempt
(no doubt this time one of their less successful ones)
to access suitably digestible material
from whatever it was that circumstance might cast in their way –
while the cosmic force that moves the Sun and stars and so forth
carries all of us along in the flow of its unfathomable love.

14. ARMISTICE DAY CENTENARY, ODDLY ENOUGH

Aha! Something tiny is crawling across
the floor of the bathroom. Then it changes direction

when it reaches the edge of – the edge of what? – what is it? –
of a rug. What a nitwit! Can't it even tell that?

And you've no idea what life is either, have you?
Nor what the simple movement of a nearby foot could do.

15. OUR DISAPPEARING VISITORS

Late afternoon. Wandering
pretty much at random
through thick, snow-covered
dulling German woods.

Long stretches of
untouched whiteness – with suddenly
precise marks and blemishes
added here and there.

At length, every so often,
I come across the track
of a shoe-print which I
have only just learned to recognise.

Mysterious hints – left, say,
half an hour earlier
by the very same boots
that I am at present still walking in.

16. PASSING TOURISTS

Yes, well – it was touch and go – but I
decided to hang back at the intersection

where the pleasant wooded, fairly major road
was met by yet another quiet elegant foreign sidestreet

to let a left-turning car go by me first,
since all that week I had been in no great hurry.

Thus I glanced across (why not?) at the passing driver –
and she at the same moment looked back directly at me.

And I knew at once – she could have been a great deal in my life.
And I thought I saw a responsive flick of something not dissimilar.

What next? Back to a pleasant little flat, unchanged –
which she, however local, had presumably never seen –

While she went on to whatever elysian field she was going on to.

17. HOFMARKSTRASSE

A small house, almost hidden by trees, though not far from the street.
Hard to believe I shouldn't have lived there – whoever it is now does.
Can words like "death" or "boredom" ever have been spoken in such a
    place?
Could such walls ever contain a phrase like "Please get out of here!"

18. TENEMENT LIFE

Look, my fate! There's now a FOR SALE sign
in one of the windows of the flat
where (I'm almost certain – yes –
I visited them more than once)
a fairly close school-friend of mine
(though never seen since then –
not as far as I'm aware –
(not *him* by *me*, at any rate!)
– yes – well,
up there is where he used to live.
(I think.)) Certainly either in that flat
of the one just above it, where those big plants are.
(Which flat, it seems, for some secret reason,
is, most intriguingly, *not* for sale at present.)

19.

During the two weeks or so I spent there
in that captivatingly picturesque old town,
just before I went to bed
I would look out across the street –

and there would be a lamp already lit,
directly behind the same first-floor window;
a minor reassuring mystery
on every night but one.

20. A PASSING SLIGHT ORDEAL

Yet again, the bombs are falling elsewhere on the continent.
Another gorgeous bright morning outside, on the school and the park.
On a roof nearby, a seagull is keeping up a shocking long loud shriek.

21. ALL DONE IN THE PHRASING

Early morning. Still dark. Not that it greatly matters
since this new eye trouble leaves me with not much else to do
but listen to music. And thus, as the late Glenn Gould
plays (fifty years ago) a William Byrd voluntary,
an actual bird in the nearby garden releases
such a rich outburst of notes that I – involuntarily –
(although alone in the room) add a brief phrase of my own
to all this invisible here-and-there harmony.

22. NOT FORGOTTEN AFTER ALL

Morning. Sunlight. As she lies still in bed
with her back to the nearby window, the sudden shadow
of a large bird flashes across the very shoulders which, years ago,
I dreamed were wearing (probably imitation) golden wings.
I repeat her name, more loudly – and this time she wakes up.

23. NO, I AM ORPHEUS

We came out of the Underground.
I looked back to where she stood, hesitating.

"I think I'll go in here," she said –
indicating a nearby newsagent's.

"I just feel like buying one of those
rubbishy fashion magazines."

24. MORE OR LESS

Since there was still an hour more or less to be got through
before her yoga lesson in the Neighbourhood Leisure Centre ended,
I made my way off alone to the nearby Park
to look again at the grove of fossilised roots of trees
which have stood there for the last 330 million years, more or less.

25. THE RIGHT [TO] LIFE

So there it was. 150 million years
of flashing about this planet – (highly unconvincingly,
if I may say so now) – and all to accomplish what?

(I can't even remember how long ago they died out!)

On we go. A few traces remain of them – and many more
are no doubt still to be found – if anyone ever finds them.
If anyone happens to dig about in exactly the right places –

(which is by no means inevitable. Or even necessary as such.)

But as for what any of these sublime beings may have thought
(are we to assume nothing?) about this perfectly unrun business,
or what reason there could possibly be (so to speak) *behind it all* –

(or time, or the right [to] life, or the helpful flight of angels –)

anything much beyond 'Sunlight – Food – Another of my species!
I'm able to do it! Yes! Yes – I'm about to. In fact – it's being done!'
seems somewhat elusive to us, endless day after endless night

(without even the high-class concepts of *life* and *death* to help out?)

But now all that, whatever it was, is pretty much something else –
with a quaver or two not yet lost of that measureless dissonance
which (let me guess) must have made up an even greater volume

than all the (much more) significant noises that are being made now.

Yes. Loving words. Witty, cruel or irrelevant words. (And so on.)
Music. Or cries of pain. Joy. Or these traffic noises outside.
The sudden ring of a doorbell. So many doors in time

opening and closing – with or without a world-cancelling slam.